The Mean Giant

words by Jill McDougall
illustrated by Grant Wilson

"What is in your barn?" yelled the mean giant.

"My cart," said the little girl.

"What is in your cart?" yelled the mean giant.

"My bag," said the little girl.

"What is in your bag?" yelled the mean giant.

"My mirror,"
said the little girl.

"What is in your mirror?" yelled the mean giant.

"Look," said the little girl.

"Help! It is a mean giant," yelled the mean giant.